resolved
to follow Christ

52 Biblical Reflections & Resolutions

Mike Fabarez

Resolved to Follow Christ
Fifty-two Biblical Reflections & Resolutions

ISBN 978-0-9816293-5-3

For information on this publication please contact:

Focal Point Radio Ministries
P.O. Box 2850
Laguna Hills, CA 92654
(888) 320-5885
FocalPointMinistries.org

Preface

Vows, promises, pledges, commitments and resolves have played an important and enduring role in God's economy. Men and women in the Bible and throughout church history have made good use of resolute statements and prayers, which God's Spirit has capitalized on to change lives, influence the world and propagate the gospel.

I encourage you to use this fifty-two week devotional to not only ponder and reflect on the biblical truths that are presented, but to also decide that you will thoughtfully follow and engage in the fifty-two resolutions that accompany each week's devotion.

I have also provided a reading schedule for each week, which if followed will take you through the entire Bible, both Old and New Testaments in one year.

I trust that as you contemplate the greatness of God and the depth of his grace your heart will be eager to respond to his word with determination and resolve.

-- Pastor Mike

Remember, O Lord, in David's favor,
all the hardships he endured,
how he swore to the Lord
and vowed to the Mighty One of Jacob
(Psalm 132:1-2)

The Words of God

And we also thank God constantly for this, that when you received the word of God, which you heard from us, you accepted it not as the word of men but as what it really is, the word of God, which is at work in you believers.
1 Thessalonians 2:13

As C. S. Lewis said concerning Jesus' claims (i.e. he is either a lunatic, a liar or Lord), so something similar could be said about the choices we face when we consider the book in which those claims are recorded.

Either the Bible is a collection of error-laced letters penned by delusional authors who thought they saw and heard things that never really happened, adding interpretations of would-be events which they believed, but which had no correspondence with reality. Or the book is a shrewdly crafted hoax intended to mislead people to believe in things that the authors knew were not accurate or true. Or the Bible is a record of God's revelation, penned by the means of honest men of sound mind who did not, and would not, embellish or distort the revelation they were conveying.

The latter is precisely the claim that is repeatedly embedded throughout the record. Peter summarized, "no prophecy of Scripture came about by the prophet's own interpretation, for prophecy never had its origin in the will of man, but men spoke from God as they were carried along by the Holy Spirit" (2Pet.1:20-21). If the writers thought God was speaking through them when in fact he was not, instead they were delusional, then we would all be wise to throw away our Bibles and run the other way! Likewise, if the authors were trying to pull one over on us, we should be discerning enough to reject this band of liars and never again expose ourselves or our families to this kind of fraud. But if God was using these men to expose his revealed truth, then we ought to be careful to read, study, memorize and meditate on their words for in reality then, they are the words of God (1Th.2:13).

Resolve 1

I will fight the distractions that keep me from God's word and I will make reading it and studying it a top priority.

A Gift from God

*And whatever you do, in word or deed, do everything in the name
of the Lord Jesus, giving thanks to God the Father through him.
Colossians 3:17*

Working is a gift from God – a pre-fall, pre-sin, pre-curse gift. While sin's consequence injected obstacles and pain into the equation ("the ground will produce thorns" leading to work "by the sweat of your brow" – Gen.3:18, 19), the commission to work preceded the fall ("God took the man and put him in the Garden of Eden to work" – Gen.2:15).

Even in the first chapters of the Bible we are introduced to God who is said to be at "work" in creating his universe (Gen.2:2). And remember that in the perfect and blessed order of things in the New Jerusalem work is not extracted: we are told that God's "servants will serve him" (Rev.22:3).

It may be hard to believe, but even now we can experience a taste of God's perfect design for work as we adopt a new mindset concerning our labor. It is not a curse. It does not have to be drudgery. It can be a foreshadow of your eternal home. Notice the Christian perspective on work (even the most demanding work) in Paul's exhortation to the Colossians: "Slaves, obey your earthly masters in everything; and do it, not only when their eye is on you and to win their favor, but with sincerity of heart and reverence for the Lord. Whatever you do, work at it with all your heart, as working for the Lord, and not for men, since you know that you will receive your inheritance from the Lord as a reward. It is the Lord Christ you are serving" (3:22-24).

So let's stop dreading Monday morning, instead let us express a godly passion to work with all of our hearts for the glory of our King. He is coming, and he will compensate us for how we tackled our nine-to-five.

Resolve 2

I will approach my daily work mindful of its inherent worth in God's eyes, working as if Christ were the direct recipient.

Three Kinds of Prayer

*Continue steadfastly in prayer,
being watchful in it with thanksgiving.
Colossians 4:2*

There are three primary settings for biblical prayer that should have priority in our lives. The first is a focused type of scheduled prayer (Mt.6:6). This is the kind where, like Daniel's prayers three times a day or Jesus' predawn appointments, we plan to meet with God for a significant session of "pouring out our hearts before the Lord" (Ps.62:8).

The second setting for prayer is a team effort. This is when we meet with other Christians in groups to help one another direct our thoughts, intercessions and thanksgivings to God (Ac.12:11). Praying with others allows us to share one another's burdens (Gal.6:2) and prompts us to express requests and concerns to God that would have never otherwise crossed our minds.

A third setting for prayer can take place in our lives right now. It is the kind Paul called "praying continually" (1Th.5:17). These are the comments and request that should punctuate our lives as we reach out to our omnipresent God amid all the events and activities of our day (cf. Neh.2:4-5).

Let's make all three a priority as we seek to deepen our relationship and communication with the living God.

Resolve 3

I will maintain a time of focused prayer, make the effort to pray with others, and continue to talk to God hour by hour.

God's Impossibilities

*For I am sure that neither death nor life, nor angels nor rulers, nor things
present nor things to come, nor powers, nor height nor depth, nor
anything else in all creation, will be able to separate
us from the love of God in Christ Jesus our Lord.*
Romans 8:38 -39

For years on playgrounds everywhere church kids have been stymied by the agitator's questions, "Can God do anything? And if so, can he make a rock so big he can't move it?" While children may struggle with the answer, I hope the rest of us do not. Thankfully, we can offer a resounding "No!" and feel good about it – really good!

God tells us that he is a God who cannot do several things. And for that we should be eternally grateful! Consider the amazingly gracious promises he has made and inscribed for us in the pages of the Bible. All of our hope and strength regarding those promises is derived from the fact that God cannot do at least four things as it relates to those commitments.

First, God is holy and therefore is incapable of deceiving us (2Tim.2:11-13). All of his good promises are true because he could not and would not ever lie to us (Tit.1:2). Second, God is omniscient, always knowing all that can be known (Ps.139:1-6). And because he is omniscient he cannot possibly forget a promise that he has made (2Pt.3:8-9). Third, God is immutable and therefore cannot change (Mal.3:6). A gracious promise he made in 750 BC will not be rescinded because he has grown, matured, or changed over the centuries (Ps.102:25-28). Fourth, God is omnipotent, possessing all power (Jer.32:17). Therefore, all of his good promises will succeed because nothing has the power to thwart his purpose – he simply cannot fail (Rom.8:31-39).

Every promise about our future is certain and sure because God cannot be less than he is. He cannot lie, forget, change or fail! And that should provide us with a kind of confidence that engenders "strong encouragement" each and every day (Heb.6:17-19).

Resolve 4

*I will declare war on my doubts and insecurities because
God is a God who cannot lie.*

—An Appetite for Good Preaching—

*The word of the Lord remains forever. And this word is the good
news that was preached to you. So put away all malice and all
deceit and hypocrisy and envy and all slander. Like newborn infants,
long for the pure spiritual milk, that by it you may grow up into
salvation- if indeed you have tasted that the Lord is good.*
1 Peter 1:25 - 2:3

A consistent intake of challenging biblical preaching is essential for our spiritual growth. The Bible tells us that we cannot be the maturing and discerning Christians God wants us to be unless we are ingesting thoughtful biblical exposition when we gather.

Peter equated biblical preaching to the necessity of "food" in our spiritual lives (1Pet.1:25 – 2:3). The writer of Hebrews adds that if your meals are always simple and elementary you will remain infantile in your faith (Heb.5:12-14). If you hope to be a strong, astute, useful follower of Christ, biblical preaching will be a key ingredient.

While some forms of preaching may seem more palatable to our personal tastes and desires, what we truly need are sermons that challenge our thinking, lead us to honest introspection, and drive us to step up and step out for Christ in a way we never have before. While this kind of preaching may not tickle our ears, it will be the type of weekly spiritual training that will reap eternal dividends as we make growth, and not comfort, the goal of our instruction.

Resolve 5

*I will choose to value biblical preaching that challenges my mind,
convicts my spirit, and helps me be more like Christ.*

Assessing Your Prayer List

*You ask and do not receive, because you ask wrongly,
to spend it on your passions.
James 4:3*

James 4:3 diagnoses one of the most insidious problems that always undermines, and often devastates our prayer lives. The problem we're told is a kind of selfish praying, which eventually reshapes our prayer lists, turning our communication with God into little more than a personal "wish list" aimed at a less painful and a more enjoyable existence.

As James boldly warns, it is that kind of praying which God will purposefully choose to ignore. Such requests are a reflection of a kind of immature Christianity, which wrongly sees life's goal as happiness and not holiness, amusement and not ministry.

God loves to answer our prayers, but he takes no pleasure in selfishness and greed. That is why God was so complimentary of Solomon, who, when told to ask for whatever he wanted, passed on asking for riches or fame, but instead chose to ask for wisdom so that he might effectively serve God's people (1Kgs.3:1-15). God quickly responded, giving him not only what he asked for, but pouring out an abundance of blessings that would also bring Solomon happiness and joy.

So guard your prayer list from being overrun by selfish desires. Be sure to ask God for those things which will bring him glory and will make your life more useful for his cause.

Resolve 6

*I will exchange more of my simplistic, self-serving prayer
requests for those that are ministry-minded.*

Our Best Efforts

My son, if you receive my words and treasure up my commandments with you, making your ear attentive to wisdom and inclining your heart to understanding; yes, if you call out for insight and raise your voice for understanding, if you seek it like silver and search for it as for hidden treasures, then you will understand the fear of the Lord and find the knowledge of God. For the Lord gives wisdom; from his mouth come knowledge and understanding;
Proverbs 2:1-6

Second Timothy 2:15 records God's call to *"Do your best to present yourself to God as one approved, a workman who does not need to be ashamed and who correctly handles the word of truth."* This well-needed reminder shows us that accurately assessing God's direction from the Bible won't always be easy. It is open to shameful mishandling. It will require our best efforts. It will often feel like hard work.

But the good news is that the payoff is always well worth the effort. Proverbs tells us that mining God's words will be like extracting silver and taking possession of a once hidden treasure (2:1-7). The result of thoughtful, diligent and sound Bible study will end up being for us "sweeter than honey" and "more precious than gold" (Ps.19:10). So let's not believe the myth that acquiring God's mind on the issues of our lives will only require a few snippets of time and effort. Instead, let's get excited about rolling up our sleeves and pulling up a chair to fully engage our faculties in the rewarding work of biblical research.

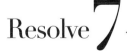

Resolve 7

I will gladly expend more effort on digging deeper into God's word, so as to diligently and accurately uncover God's thoughts.

No Idols

Little children, keep yourselves from idols.
1 John 5:21

The challenging New Testament letter of 1 John ends with the poignant summation to "keep yourself from idols" (5:21). While our minds may revert to flannel graph images of bearded ancients bowing down to metallic statues, it is important to recognize that "idolatry" from a biblical perspective is a competing devotion to any priority that supplants, challenges or threatens our commitment and allegiance to God.

While we don't encounter our friends and coworkers prostrate before golden images, we can't help but see the myriad of alluring pursuits that work to squeeze out the supremacy of Christ in everyday life. So perhaps now more than ever we must be vigilant to "keep ourselves from idols."

Let's make sure that Jesus and his Lordship come first and everything else is a distant second.

Resolve 8

I will consider all the things that I love and guard against them ever becoming a greater love and priority than Christ.

— Counterintuitive Thanksgiving—

*Give thanks in all circumstances; for this is the will
of God in Christ Jesus for you.
1 Thessalonians 5:18*

First Thessalonians 5:18 requires that Christians "give thanks in all circumstances." While to some this may seem crazy or at least a strange kind of spiritual masochism, the Bible has good reason for directing us to be grateful even when life hurts.

For starters, Christians affirm that God is sovereign and has good intentions when he enlists trials and pain in the lives of the children he deeply loves. As we parents interact with our young children (assuming we are humble enough to accept that *we* are God's "kids") we should quickly recognize that pain is often a strategic path to healing, maturity, and prosperity in this world. If only our kids could see through their immaturity that the bad tasting medicine, the hassle of homework, or the sting of discipline will eventually yield great benefit, then perhaps they, like us, could learn to complain less and even find the strength to be grateful in the face of circumstances that are less than fun.

May God give us the maturity to "give thanks" in good times and bad.

Resolve 9

*Instead of complaining during the next painful circumstance, I
will consider God's potential purposes and choose to give thanks.*

——The Deception of Laziness——

The soul of the sluggard craves and gets nothing,
while the soul of the diligent is richly supplied.
Proverbs 13:4

In the Book of Proverbs God poignantly underscores the harm associated with laziness. Even the word translated in our Bibles to describe such people carries a stinging admonition. God calls us "sluggards" when we fall into patterns of being undisciplined, idle or unduly lethargic.

"That's not me" we may be quick to say, but Proverbs insightfully points out that it is hard for "the sluggard" to see his own problem. One reason is because "the sluggard" is a master of excuses. When we're lazy we can make up millions of reasons for not doing what we know we should (Pr.22:13; 26:13). Add to that "the sluggard" is said to be "wiser in his own eyes than seven men who can answer discreetly" (Pr.26:16). Pride often keeps us from admitting that we have settled for an undisciplined lifestyle.

When laziness is true of us, God wants us to own it (Pr.6:9). He would have us see that many of the unpleasant circumstances in our lives are no one's fault but our own (Pr.15:19).

May God, in his grace, create in us a spirit like that of his Son. May we be known for our discipline, diligence and willingness to do our "work with all of our hearts, as working for the Lord" (Col.3:23).

——Resolve 10——

I will make laziness my enemy and I will recommit myself to
working with diligence, discipline and excellence.

Reigning in Our Words

*For we all stumble in many ways. And if anyone does not
stumble in what he says, he is a perfect man, able also
to bridle his whole body.*
James 3:2

The Bible says that if we can control what we say,
everything else is a snap (cf. Jms.3:2). When it comes to our
fallen humanity, nothing is more depraved than our mouths.
The Bible says that our tongue is "a fire" and "a world of evil
among the parts of the body" (Jms.3:6a). God says it can "set
the whole course of our lives on fire" and he even goes so far
as to say that our tongues are "set on fire by hell" (v.6b). Wow!
Talk about a wake up call. God wants us to be sure we realize
how much trouble our words can cause.

It is because of this potential damage that the Bible
gives us some very practical advice. Simply put, talk less! Or
at least we should make sure we pause and think hard before
we start talking. In the words of the first chapter of James, we
should "keep a tight rein" on our words and always be "slow to
speak" (vv.26 & 19).

So no matter who you are or where you're at in the
Christian life, it is always a good idea to recommit yourself to
policing your words and asking for God's help in governing
your mouth.

Resolve 11

*I will work to govern my mouth, I will choose to say less, and I
will decide ahead of time to speak words that are helpful.*

—— Guarding Against Greed ——

But godliness with contentment is great gain, for we brought nothing into the world, and we cannot take anything out of the world. But if we have food and clothing, with these we will be content.
1 Timothy 6:6-8

Most of us, at one point or another, have said in frustration, "I hate money!" While that may sound better than the alternative which is prohibited in Scripture (1Tim.6:10), it is obviously not how God would have us live.

God knows we will have to function in a world run with money. He also knows we will encounter all the problems and temptations that come with it. But God would have us master this potentially unruly aspect of life and not be mastered by it. "Master it," not by achieving some kind of "independently wealthy" status, but by working with God's Spirit to keep all its related temptations and frustrations from taking hold of our hearts. Because, as many can testify, a bigger income doesn't neutralize money's problem – it usually magnifies it! The biblical goal is contentment!

True contentment may be an illusive aspect of godliness, but, as Paul wrote, it holds the promise of real "gain" (1Tim.6:6). Contentment is antithetical to worry, anxiety, greed and covetousness. That alone should provide us with ample motivation. So today, let's take stock of the gifts God has given. Let us, with God's help, untangle our hearts from the discouragement and pain that comes from a heightened focus on our financial challenges. Let us live self-controlled and contented lives that trust in God and not the things that he provides.

—— Resolve 12 ——

I will aim at contentment, being truly thankful for what God has given me, and remaining on guard against every form of greed.

———— # Careful to be Thankful ————

I will give thanks to the Lord with my whole heart;
I will recount all of your wonderful deeds.
Psalm 9:1

Like Nebuchadnezzar strutting on the walls of Babylon (Dan.4), or Herod taking his bows in royal robes (Ac.12), or the nine former lepers thoughtlessly strolling on their merry way (Lk.17), when moderns carelessly deny God the credit for their origins or their daily blessings they cannot think that they will be exempt from divine displeasure.

Certainly God, above all others, deserves credit for his works. The Bible does not remember Nebuchadnezzar, Herod and the nine former lepers as self-made role models, but as warnings. They are reminders that when the Creator decides to bless our lives and our world with beauty, pleasure or prosperity we, as his creatures, should always take the time to humbly praise him for being the gracious Giver.

The Psalmist tells us to "Give thanks to the Lord, call on his name; make known among the nations what he has done. Sing to him, sing praise to him; tell of all his wonderful acts" (Ps.105:1-2). Let's embrace that directive, open our eyes to God's works and boldly give him the credit for the great things he has done.

———————————— Resolve **13** ————

I will be more conscious of God's daily blessings and be quick to thank him for every good thing he bestows on my life.

Making Rough Places Plane

Pray then like this: Our Father in heaven,
hallowed be your name.
Your kingdom come, your will be done,
on earth as it is in heaven.
Matthew 6:9-10

The biblical concept of "sin" has rightly been described as an aberration or deviation from the way things ought to be. Part of being "salt and light" in this world (Mt.5:13-16) is to strategically say and do the kinds of things in any given situation that help to make the world more like what God intended it to be.

While it is true that God will one day bring everything in the universe in line with what is absolutely right (1Cor.15:24-25), in the meantime we should seek to follow the lead of God's Spirit to do what we can to see more of "his will" realized here on earth, like it is now in heaven (Mt.6:10). So whether it's in our homes, offices or neighborhoods let us thoughtfully and prayerfully exert a kind of redemptive influence that will move things from the way they are to the way they ought to be.

It may not always be awarded and rewarded in this life, but God will be honored and you will give those around you a foretaste of Christ's kingdom of which we pray they will one day be a part.

Resolve 14

I will purpose to be salt and light in this world, restraining evil
whenever possible and seeking to establish more of what is right.

Making the Time

*And rising very early in the morning, while it was still dark, he
departed and went out to a desolate place, and there he prayed.
Mark 1:35*

Few would disagree that life is busy and cluttered with activity. Even so, it is imperative that we follow the pattern set for us by Christ, regularly shutting out everything to quietly spend time in communion and fellowship with God. This was the habit of Jesus' life. Luke tells us that he "often withdrew to lonely places and prayed" (Lk.5:16).

While that may seem unrealistic with our hectic schedules, it is important to remember the many things and the multitudes of people who were always trying to force their way into Christ's schedule. It is also helpful to realize that Jesus had to work hard to make these solitary encounters happen. He didn't just happen to "have the time," Jesus "made the time" as they say. For example, Mark records that "very early in the morning, while it was still dark, Jesus got up, left the house and went off to a solitary place, where he prayed" (Mk.1:35). Matthew tells us that at other times he needed to stay up late into the night to find any quiet time to pray (Mt.14:23-25).

I know it is hard, and I know we like our sleep, but alone time with God is the most important investment we can make in the next twenty-four hours.

Resolve 15

I will not be a victim of a busy life, I will schedule time with God, consistently keep it, and vigorously guard it.

God's Grace

For the grace of God has appeared,
bringing salvation for all people,
training us to renounce ungodliness and worldly passions,
and to live self-controlled, upright,
and godly lives in the present age
Titus 2:11-12

God's grace is the theme of the New Testament, and yet with all this scriptural emphasis it seems we are still slow to rightly understand it. We either tend to think that grace is some kind of extra credit that adds to our goodness, thus making us acceptable to God. Or we secretly tend to believe it is a "get out of jail free" card that allows us to dabble in sin without consequences. Both of these views are a perversion of what is presented to us in God's word.

Biblical grace is the immeasurable and completely unearned favor that God grants to us because of Christ and in spite of ourselves. It is not an add-on, but a complete replacement of our attempts at earning a place in God's family. Once granted, God's grace is tenacious in instructing us to deny ungodliness and live holy lives – not to earn God's favor, but in response to it (Tit.2:12).

Let us always be grateful for grace, being careful to understand it as we should.

Resolve 16

I will celebrate God's grace as reason for my complete acceptance
before God, and be careful to respond to it by striving to be holy.

—— Determined to be Helpful ——

Blessed be the God and Father of our Lord Jesus Christ,
the Father of mercies and God of all comfort,
who comforts us in all our affliction,
so that we may be able to comfort those
who are in any affliction, with the comfort
with which we ourselves are comforted by God.
2 Corinthians 1:3-4

Most of us prefer to live on a cul-de-sac. We tend to like them because they allow us the tranquility of forgoing all the unnecessary traffic running through our lives. After all, the main streets allow way too much congestion coming our way that ultimately has its business elsewhere.

Unfortunately when it comes to our spiritual lives God hasn't called us to the serenity of a cul-de-sac, he's designed us to be a busy and productive conduit. While we'd naturally prefer the tranquility of decisions and investments that only benefit me and mine, God has called us to suffer the hardships and hassles of involvement for the good of others.

So when you're deciding whether or not to go to that service, get involved in that program or attend that church event, remember that it may not be about *your* edification! It may very well be that God wants to bring that experience into your life so that you can be equipped, positioned or prepared to be a blessing to someone else. And as this happens may we remember the words of Jesus that it is indeed "more blessed to give than to receive" (Ac.20:35).

—— Resolve 17 ——

I will no longer assess my opportunities exclusively in terms of what they will provide me, I will also consider how I can help.

Sharing with a Purpose

You also must help us by prayer,
so that many will give thanks on our behalf
for the blessing granted us through the prayers of many.
2 Corinthians 1:11

When you are on the fence about whether to share your trial, your hurt, or your burden with a brother or sister in Christ, be sure to remember the words of 2 Corinthians 1:11. The Apostle Paul would have us know that when we keep our struggles to ourselves we bypass God's ordained support system for our lives and we even deprive God of a measure of praise that he would otherwise receive.

Second Corinthians 1:11 tells us that we are truly "helped" by the prayers of our fellow disciples. For Paul, his despair (v.8) was transformed into hope and perseverance (v.10)! Genuine strength and sustenance is granted to us because of the intercession of God's people. More importantly, 2 Corinthians 1:11 goes on to say that when the prayer circle for our hurts and trials is broadened, there are more Christians who end up giving thanks to God when his gracious answer to our team-praying is finally provided.

So if you are in the middle of a difficult problem, go ahead and confide in your brothers and sisters in Christ, and be sure not to go it alone!

Resolve 18

I will stop keeping all my difficulties and trials to myself, instead I
will honestly and humbly seek the help of my fellow Christians.

Planning

*The plans of the diligent lead surely to abundance,
but everyone who is hasty comes only to poverty.*
Proverbs 21:25

The Bible has a lot to say about God's "good purpose" (Phil.2:13; Heb.6:17). It seems that on every other page we read of another instance of God working out his predetermined plan (Eph.1:9-11).

As Christians, it would be hard to reflect the virtues of God without being a man or a woman with a "planner" in hand. We see in Scripture that a godly person is one who "plans to work then works the plan" as they say (cf. 2Cor.1:17). All too often we don't accomplish half of the good that we could, not because we fail to work, but because we fail to plan.

So be sure to stop in a quiet place today or tomorrow and write down the answers to these simple questions: *"What good should I do for the glory of Christ? ...this week? ...this month? ...this year?"* You might find that as God enables you to "work the plan" that you have actually accomplished far more for his glory than you could have ever asked or imagined (cf. Eph.3:18-21).

Resolve 19

I will work to plan, plan to work, and then work the plan - so that by God's grace I might be maximally productive for Jesus Christ.

19

Shine

You are the light of the world. A city set on a hill cannot be hidden. Nor do people light a lamp and put it under a basket, but on a stand, and it gives light to all in the house. In the same way, let your light shine before others, so that they may see your good works and give glory to your Father who is in heaven.
Matthew 5:14-16

Jesus makes it clear; he has no interest in "covert Christians." He expects our commitment to him to "shine" forth in everything we do. He has no tolerance for tasteless garnish and lamps with opaque shades (Mt.5:14-15). He says that Christians who blend in are "good for nothing" (v.13). It is no surprise that Jesus was not impressed with Nicodemus who wanted to chat with the Christ under the cover of darkness (Jn.3:2). Jesus knows that our standing up and standing out will make a difference for eternity, as those rightly affected will one day "praise our Father in heaven" (Mt.5:16).

So if it's possible that those around you don't know why you live, think and talk the way you do, be sure to fill them in that you have been changed, and that you will continue to change, because you have become a follower of Christ.

Resolve 20

I will work to make sure that those with whom I have regular contact know that I am a devoted follower of Jesus Christ.

Top Priority

For I am not ashamed of the gospel,
for it is the power of God for salvation
to everyone who believes,
to the Jew first and also to the Greek.
Romans 1:16

God's desire is to see people repent of their sins and place their trust in Jesus Christ. Nothing in all the world could be more urgent or important. Amazingly, God has granted us the privilege of being the avenue through which he does this work.

When we consider the immense ramifications of this life-changing transaction, we quickly realize that none of our life's activities or accomplishments will compare with the honor of being used to bring someone into the family of God. With that in view, it makes sense that the Apostle Paul would say that he did not see his life of any real value unless he was faithful to "testify to the gospel of the grace of God" (Ac.20:24).

Of course there are several important things we can do this week, but all of them will pale by comparison to the eternal importance of proclaiming the saving message of Christ and his call to repentance and faith. So don't let good things squeeze out the important. Don't allow "better" things to keep you from doing what is best. Set your sights on representing God and his gospel.

Resolve 21

I will look for opportunities to share the gospel and when I see them I will boldly tell people about the good news of Jesus Christ.

Get Up!

For the righteous falls seven times and rises again,
but the wicked stumble in times of calamity.
Proverbs 24:16

Because of God's grace, our lives are full of potential usefulness for Jesus Christ. God has a proven track record of consistently reaching out to restore his stumbling servants.

Proverbs 24:16 compares the "falling" of two kinds of people – those who get up and those who don't. Thankfully, as Jesus demonstrated by extending forgiveness and restoration to Peter after his threefold denial (Jn.21), God's mercy and grace extend to his people in order to stand them up, dust them off, and move them forward into productive and fruitful Christian lives.

God wants your life to count. He wants you to make a difference for someone this week. So if your focus is on yesterday's failures, get a biblical perspective: agree with God about your sin, affirm his promise of forgiveness and say to him, "Here am I, send me" (Is.6:6-8).

Resolve 22

After I confess a sin and repent of it, I will choose to boldly move
forward trusting God's grace that I will be useful for him today.

Attitude Adjustment

And let us consider how to stir up one another to love and good
works, not neglecting to meet together, as is the habit of some,
but encouraging one another, and all the
more as you see the Day drawing near.
Hebrews 10:24-25

When, in Psalm 73, the psalmist finds himself frustrated by his daily struggles, and aggravated by the inequities of life, it is amazing how quickly and simply his angst is resolved. This is especially true when we begin to sympathize with the depth of his annoyance. He says, "all day long" he is "plagued," "grieved" and "embittered." Those are strong words to which most of us can relate when life gets tough and we run into harsh disappointments.

The fix? It is simpler than we might imagine. The psalmist confesses that the turnaround came when he "entered the sanctuary of God" (v.17). He speaks of a profound and needed adjustment in his perspective as he encounters God and God's people in a place of worship.

Remember that while many may view church as an extracurricular activity, it is in reality God's essential prescription to keep our lives, our hearts, and our emotions out of the gutter. With that in mind, we'd be wise to reaffirm our commitment to never "give up on meeting together" at church each week (Heb.10:25).

Resolve 23

I will make church a top priority and take every opportunity to
meaningfully connect with God's people.

——— Making Each Day Count ———

So teach us to number our days
that we may get a heart of wisdom.
Psalm 90:12

Talk about perspective! The lyrics of Psalm 39 boldly prompt the worshipper to consider the brief nature of his or her time here on earth. Verses four and five read: *Oh Lord, make me know my end and what is the measure of my days; let me know how fleeting I am! Behold, you have made my days a few handbreadths, and my lifetime is as nothing before you.*

While that may be a depressing part of the Bible for our youth-idolizing culture, God isn't trying to make us feel bad, his goal here and elsewhere is to get us to reprioritize our lives and motivate us to invest wisely in the days we have left. Consider the book of Ecclesiastes, which reminds us that our short lives are often wasted chasing after things that, in the end, amount to nothing.

Today, it is variously reported that the average American lifespan is approximately 75 years. That's only about 27,394 days. It is enlightening to do the math and see how many days you have already spent and how many days you might expect (but not presume) to have left on this journey.

If you do the math, don't get depressed! Instead, get motivated to make each remaining day count. Let us consciously invest in things that matter for eternity. May this daring perspective drive us to step up and make a difference for Christ this week!

——— Resolve 24 ———

I will think often of the fact that this life is fleeting and my days on earth are few, so that I might maximize each day for Christ.

The Great Escape

And no creature is hidden from his sight,
but all are naked and exposed to the eyes of him
to whom we must give account.
Hebrews 4:13

Proverbs 29:25 says that the "fear of man will prove to be a snare." Unfortunately, this is a trap that catches us often. While it may be hard to resist, the Bible tells us that a life constrained by the fear of what people will think of us or may do to us, is a life destined for compromise and defeat (1Pt.3:14). Instead, the Bible consistently calls the righteous to be "as bold as a lion" (Prov.28:1).

Vanquishing the fear of man can only be attained by having a proper and healthy fear of God. Jesus told us that if our fear of God is what it ought to be, we won't fear what people can do to us even if they were to take all that we have (Mt.10:28). God is our ultimate authority. He is the One to whom we will answer. In the long run, pleasing him is all that really matters.

Set your sights on living for an audience of One and you will find that you're avoiding the pain and encumbrance of Proverbs 29:25.

Resolve 25

I will live for an audience of One, remembering that it is
God to whom I must give an account.

No Solitary Christians

But God, who comforts the downcast, comforted us by the coming of Titus, and not only by his coming but also by the comfort with which he was comforted by you, as he told us of your longing, your mourning, your zeal for me, so that I rejoiced still more.
2 Corinthians 7:6-7

There is too much spiritual danger inherent in Christians choosing to be isolated. The New Testament model shows us Christians who are interested and involved in each other's lives.

Paul shared his joys and victories, as well as his hurts and struggles with his friends. He was transparent about his pain, even to the point of telling the Corinthians that at one point he "despaired even of life" (2Cor.1:8). When he was weak, he not only cried out to God, but he also called out for the help of his Christian friends. "Come to me quickly" he told Timothy, because he was left without the support of those he formerly trusted (2Tim.4:9). And when he openly sought the needed fellowship of his spiritual family, he saw the hand of God and felt the encouragement of the Holy Spirit in their voices and consolation: "God, who comforts the downcast, comforted us with the coming of Titus" (2Cor.7:6). When Paul sat with his Christian comrades, he wasn't trying to keep up some kind of super-spiritual appearance, he was there as a real, vulnerable and transparent follower of Christ.

We would do well to follow this biblical pattern. Spiritual trouble finds its fuel when we choose to be isolated. So reach out and be real. Seek to serve and be served. Look for the mutual encouragement and support that comes when real Christians truly get to know and love each other.

Resolve 26

I will risk being vulnerable and transparent with other Christians, knowing I cannot afford to be isolated.

Whose Reputation?

Do not be surprised, brothers, that the world hates you.
1 John 3:13

Obedience to Christ often comes down to whose reputation we care about the most. When God calls us to stand up for what is right, speak up for what is important, or be counted with his children, the price will usually be debited from our reputation. On the other hand, obedience to God will promote the reputation of Christ. How many times have we refrained from the "right thing" because we were afraid of what people would think? But had we stepped up or spoken out, we would have in some way advanced the glory of Christ. Jesus is the ultimate example of obedience at the cost of acceptance and popularity.

Christ was singularly focused on the glory of the Father (Jn.17:4), but it led to increasing opposition, betrayal and rejection. Jesus knew his followers would wish for an exemption. But the principle highlighted by Christ's obedience can be expected in our own lives. At one point Jesus had to draw what should have been an obvious comparison: "If the world hates you, keep in mind it hated me first. No servant is greater than his master. If they persecuted me, they will persecute you also" (Jn.15:18, 20).

So when we are faced with doing right and are afraid it may cause us problems, we need to remind ourselves that we are to care more about the glory of God than our own glory. We need to clarify that we should value the advancement of Christ more than our own advancement. We should resolve that Christ's reputation is more important than our own.

Lastly, we must remember that the injustice will be short-lived. One day God will eternally honor those who honored him (1Sam.2:30). He will purpose to serve those who served his cause (Lk.12:37). While the world may shun us, ridicule us and persecute us, we know that "our light and momentary troubles are achieving for us an eternal glory that far outweighs them all" (2Cor.4:17).

Resolve 27

I will care more about what the God of heaven thinks of me, rather than what the people of this world think of me.

Thoughtful Love

*Love one another with brotherly affection. Outdo one
another in showing honor.*
Romans 12:10

The book of Proverbs sets before us several thought provoking and inspired truths that can and should have a significant impact on how we "wisely" relate to one another. Take for instance the curious and seemingly obvious proverb that reads: "If a man loudly blesses his neighbor early in the morning, it will be taken as a curse" (Pr.27:14).

Consider how often our judgment is skewed by our own set of personal preferences, propensities and inclinations. In our subjectivity, we tend to think that if we would appreciate "this or that" so would everyone else. But this is clearly not the case. This becomes obvious when people from various backgrounds and different ages seek to live harmoniously in the body of Christ. And, of course, who can overstate this proverb's importance amid the challenges of marriage and parenting? We are not all the same. What I would consider an act of love or encouragement may not be received as such by someone else.

Real Christian love is a thoughtful endeavor. We must work to care for one another with an intelligent and considerate love. "How will this be received?" "What would really be understood as helpful to him?" "How does she respond to this kind of encouragement?" These are the kinds of critical questions we must ask ourselves. More than avoiding the obvious (e.g., morning people shouldn't call night owls at 7 AM and men shouldn't give tools as anniversary gifts), we should seek to be skillful in the way we relate to one another. This will please God and will make the church and our homes what God intended them to be.

Resolve 28

*I will thoughtfully consider the best way to encourage, correct, or
help other people, remembering not everyone is like me.*

Don't Give Up

Therefore, my beloved brothers, be steadfast, immovable,
always abounding in the work of the Lord,
knowing that in the Lord your labor is not in vain.
1 Corinthians 15:58

In a world that rarely rewards truly good behavior, it is not a surprise that God's people would be tempted to grow weary in doing what is right. But we shouldn't. The Bible calls us to constantly renew our perspective and our strength, remembering that doing the right thing is always the right thing.

After reminding us that "sowing and reaping" is an unwavering reality (even if the sprouts of consequence are long in coming), Paul calls the Galatian churches to *"not become weary in doing good, for in the proper time we will reap a harvest if we do not give up"* (Gal.6:9). We must not forget that God is on the throne and that he will inevitably reward righteous behavior. Don't give up. Don't despair. Keep faithfully following his path and upholding his precepts. In the end he will vindicate every good deed.

In the meantime, look to him for strength. He can give you the perseverance you need. "The Lord gives strength to his people" (Ps.29:11) and God "increases the power of the weak" (Is.40:29). So ask him today for the courage, the power and the perspective to keep doing what's right regardless of what others may say. In time we will see it was all worth it.

Resolve 29

I will fight any temptation that distracts me from confidently
believing that persevering in doing good is always worth it.

——— Important Preparation ———

For the word of God is living and active, sharper than any two-edged sword, piercing to the division of soul and of spirit, of joints and of marrow, and discerning the thoughts and intentions of the heart.
Hebrews 4:12

Responding appropriately to God's word, whether it is being read or it is being preached, requires an important preparatory step that is often neglected. God's word is said to be "living and active" and sufficiently able to have a transforming impact on our lives (Heb.4:12; Jer.23:29; Jn.17:17).

Often the difference between the times it impacts our lives and the times it doesn't, Jesus told us, is not a question of the quality of the word, but a problem with the receptivity of the heart (Lk.8:15). Being receptive requires some prep. So before we open the Scriptures in church or at our kitchen tables, we would do well to echo the words of King David who prayed, "Search me, O God, and know my heart! Try me and know my thoughts! And see if there be any grievous way in me, and lead me in the way everlasting" (Ps.139:23-24). That kind of prayerful prelude to any encounter with God's word can dissolve our stubbornness, soften our defenses, and eliminate any obstinate resistance we may have to being transformed by his truth. It is a simple yet vulnerable step, which will yield tremendous dividends in our lives.

Therefore, let us always be careful to prepare to welcome the Lord's truth, accepting it "not as the word of men but as what it really is, the word of God, which is at work" in us (1Th.2:13).

——— Resolve 30 ———

I will stop and prayerfully prepare my heart before I read, study or listen to God's word being taught.

—— The Supremacy of Wisdom ——

If any of you lacks wisdom, let him ask God,
who gives generously to all without reproach,
and it will be given him.
James 1:5

There is a big difference between intelligence and wisdom. There are many intelligent people who are utterly devoid of wisdom and many wise men and women who didn't fare well on the SATs. Wisdom is described in the Bible as the skill of living life as God intended. It is not just the ability to "think well" but rather to "thoughtfully act" in a way that is good and godly.

Our wisdom is tested every day, not with exams that evaluate our mental dexterity, but with the options we face regarding our behavior, values and conversation. The Bible asks, "Who is wise and understanding among you? Let him show it by his good life, by deeds done in the humility that comes from wisdom" (Jms.3:13).

It is admirable to strive to increase your intelligence, but it is far more important to make progress in acquiring wisdom. Solomon exhorted us to "Get wisdom… though it costs you all you have" because "wisdom is supreme" (Pr.4:7). It begins with a right perspective of God (Pr.9:10) and is increased by time in God's word (Ps.119:99). Let's all seek more of it, for God loves to grant it.

—— Resolve 31 ——

I will show the value I place on wisdom by diligently pursuing it
and praying regularly that God will grant more of it to me.

—— Important Preparation ——

I have seen everything that is done under the sun,
and behold, all is vanity and a striving after wind.
Ecclesiastes 1:14

While the world holds out the promise of happiness, fulfillment and satisfaction, the Bible warns us not to believe it. We live in a world system that tries desperately to convince us that if we just had a little more of what the world offers over here, or what the world can provide us over there, then we would be truly joyful and happy.

The entire advertising industry works from this premise. They tell us to just imagine ourselves in the next car, moving in to a new neighborhood, on the next vacation, or clutching the next new gadget, then, they say, we will truly experience real living. It is then, they promise, that our hearts will be at rest, our desires will be fulfilled and our lives will be complete. We should know by now it's just not so.

God was careful to include in his inspired library the ultimate "been-there-done that" exhortation. It's called the book of Ecclesiastes, and if you have read it lately you know that no matter how much you're tempted to buy the world's line about real living and true happiness, God tells us we must not believe it. It is a lie that will only disappoint.

As Augustine rightly said, "God has made us for himself, and our hearts are restless until we find rest in him." Paul, in his poignant manner declares, "The world is crucified to me, and I to the world" (Gal.6:14). As Asaph sang, "Whom have I in heaven but you, and earth has nothing I desire besides you" (Ps.73:25). So let's look past the empty lies of our world, and pursue with diligence the only reality that can grant us fulfillment, joy, satisfaction and peace.

—— Resolve 32 ——

I refuse to believe that a little more of what the world has to offer will
fulfill my heart, which in reality is designed to be filled by God.

Convicted

And do not grieve the Holy Spirit of God,
by whom you were sealed for the day of redemption.
Ephesians 4:30

It is our natural fallen tendency to make excuses. Our human propensity is to try to squirm out from under the weight of all those unpleasant feelings, concerning what we are doing or saying and when we are pondering something unrighteous or unholy. Because sanctification is a process, and because perfect personal holiness will not be achieved until we reach our glorified state in a resurrected body, the daily feelings of conviction will abound in our Christian lives. We will feel all varieties of large and small pangs of guilt for our less than holy words, actions and attitudes.

Not only do we have a conscience, which is given to all people for such a purpose, but as Christians we have our conscience kicked into turbo drive because of the regenerative work of the Holy Spirit, beginning at the point of our repentance and faith in Christ. More than that, God himself has invaded our lives and his holy presence will ensure that God's "hand is heavy upon us" when we fail to deal with our sin (Ps.32:3-4).

How we respond to these daily pangs, which are intended to drive us toward increasing holiness is obviously at the heart of spiritual growth. How can we grow spiritually and become more like Christ while failing to own up to and confess the sins that entangle our minds, words and actions? God has saved us irrespective of our holiness (Eph.2:8; Tit.3:5), but he saves us so that we might live holy lives (Tit.2:14; 1Pt.1:15). And being responsive to the Spirit's conviction is key.

Resolve 33

I will pay closer attention to pangs of guilt in order to assess whether or not they are rightly identifying sin that needs my attention.

33

The Next Life

If then you have been raised with Christ,
seek the things that are above, where Christ is,
seated at the right hand of God.
Set your minds on things that are above,
not on things that are on earth.
For you have died, and your life is hidden
with Christ in God.
When Christ who is your life appears,
then you also will appear with him in glory.
Colossians 3:1-4

Part of the reason God gave us divine revelation about the next life is to motivate us in this one. Some have said Christians can be "so heavenly minded, they are no earthly good." But as C.S. Lewis rightly pointed out, Christians are no earthly good until they are heavenly minded. Until we digest what God says about the end of this world and the beginning of the next, we will never truly embrace Christ's values or live a Christ-like life.

The New Testament repeatedly drives this point home, frequently exhorting us to "set our hearts on things above" (Col.3:1-2). Jesus calls us to punctuate our prayers with an ardent request for God's "kingdom to come" (Mt.6:10).

Because our decisions, our discussions and our disposition need that eternal perspective, may God empower us today to "fix our eyes not on what is seen, but on what is unseen, for what is seen is temporary, but what is unseen is eternal" (2Cor.4:18).

Resolve 34

I will set my mind, heart and expectation on the day when the
kingdoms of the world will become the kingdom of our Lord.

Craftsmanship

*Worthy are you, our Lord and God,
to receive glory and honor and power,
for you created all things, and by your will
they existed and were created."
Revelation 4:11*

While many of us affirm the truth that God made the world and that it displays his handiwork, and while some of us go so far as to say that it is God's strategic source of "general revelation" to mankind, it is unfortunate that most of us take so little time to utilize God's creation as a catalyst for worship.

David states that "the heavens declare the glory of God and the skies proclaim the work of his hand... day after day they pour forth speech and night after night they display knowledge" (Ps.19:1-2). That was not just a theological assertion for David, it was most often a stirring prompt to pray, sing and worship the Creator.

In Psalm 8 for instance, David recognized the various ways God's greatness is seen in the created order (from the stars and the moon to the varieties of herds, birds and fish) only to frame his observations with heartfelt praise: "O Lord, our Lord, how majestic is your name in all the earth" (vv.1, 9).

While the world is often enamored with God's creation, yet failing to honor the Creator (Rom.1:25), let us not miss the daily opportunities given to us through the sunsets, constellations or crisp ocean air to specifically and sincerely praise the Creator whose craftsmanship is on perpetual display.

Resolve35

I will look to God's creation with a heightened awareness of the many reasons I have to praise him.

Real Confession

*For godly grief produces a repentance that leads to salvation
without regret, whereas worldly grief produces death.
For see what earnestness this godly grief has produced in you, but also
what eagerness to clear yourselves, what indignation,
what fear, what longing, what zeal, what punishment!
At every point you have proved yourselves innocent in the matter.*
2 Corinthians 7:10-11

The Bible instructs us to "confess" our sins (1Jn.1:9). While many think that means to say "I'm sorry" to God, the word actually precludes most forms of modern apologies.

The word confess in the Greek New Testament is a compound word which is made up of the words "the same" and "to speak". The idea is that when we confess our sins, we say the same thing about our sins that God says. God, of course, sees our sins as detestable (2Kgs.21:11), appalling (Jer.2:12-13), shameful (Job 31:11), grievous (Eph.4:30), wicked (Gen.39:9), offensive (Pr.17:9), and even nauseating (Rev.3:16). Popular sentiments like, "I'm sorry if I offended you" or "I'm sorry you were hurt by my actions" are a long way from calling our own actions detestable or appalling.

True biblical repentance always includes seeing our sins for what they are and agreeing with God about the sinfulness of sin. That is why passages that depict biblical repentance include phrases like, "this godly sorrow has produced in you… indignation, alarm and readiness to see justice done" (2Cor.7:11).

So let us be careful that we don't mistake a half-hearted "I'm sorry" for a biblical "confession" of our sins.

Resolve 36

When I sin I will avoid simplistic apologies, choosing instead to truly agree with God about the offensiveness of my transgression.

Patient Endurance

*Not only that, but we rejoice in our sufferings, knowing that
suffering produces endurance, and endurance produces character,
and character produces hope*
Romans 5:3-4

When God led the Israelites out of Egypt, the destination was the promised land of Canaan – a land of abundance and rest. The route was through the desert – which by contrast was hot, difficult, and filled with discomfort. As is so often the case, God's good plans included a path through the desert.

From the perspective of the New Testament our entire life this side of heaven can rightly be considered a path through the desert (Jn.16:33; Ac.14:22; Heb.4:1-11; et al.). But viewed as a microcosm there are many instances in this life that follow this larger paradigm. It might be one of the many painful paths that God utilizes in our lives to bring us to a new level of maturity. It may be the discomfort of an illness before the relief of restored health. Or it might be painful financial struggles before a season of financial stability. Whatever the circumstance, we can learn from the poor example of the Israelites in their desert wanderings.

Their monumental failure was how in they handled the pain on the way to their relief. They whined and complained. They were bitter and angry. They longingly looked back at the fish and cucumbers of Egypt, instead of looking forward to the milk and honey of Canaan (Num.11:4-6).

God wants us to learn to patiently endure the hardships of our deserts with faith and hope. He has promised relief. In the meantime, his Spirit is able to make us resilient and resolute. May we not have to look back from our next "Canaan" regretting our words and our attitudes in the desert.

Resolve 37

*I will choose to stop complaining and resolve to endure whatever
difficulties I may face knowing God will eventually provide relief*

—Taking Sin and Grace Seriously—

*Brothers, I do not consider that I have made it my own. But one
thing I do: forgetting what lies behind and straining forward to
what lies ahead, I press on toward the goal for the prize
of the upward call of God in Christ Jesus.*
Philippians 3:13-14

It is not uncommon to hear people say that they have lived their lives with "no regrets". They often state that they would live just the same if they had it to do all over again. It is hard to imagine that sentiment coming from the mouth of a Christian.

While we may affirm the truth that God works all things together for good (Rom.8:28), there ought to be a true remorse for the times we have sinned against our holy and loving God. If reliving a situation were possible, I trust we would all want to amend a transgression that assailed our Savior, or maximize an opportunity to advance the cause of Christ. But the Bible is clear, we cannot.

Thankfully, our iniquities and missed opportunities have been dealt with on the cross. And God of course, would have us live in the present and not the past (Phil.3:13). He wants us to look ahead, not backwards. While our sinful histories rightly make us remorseful, the good news is that our forgiveness is complete and more opportunities to glorify Christ lie before us.

We can all admit we have regrets, but let us be quick to praise God that his grace is greater than our sin and today is a new day to live for Christ.

—Resolve 38—

*I will admit I have regrets, but I will praise God for his grace and
purpose with his help to have fewer in the days ahead.*

No More Excuses

*Now to him who is able to do far more abundantly
than all that we ask or think, according to the power at work within us
Ephesians 3:20*

When God called Moses to be his representative during a dark hour in Israel's history, Moses' response was less than compliant. We might sympathize with his reluctance to stand before Pharaoh and deliver what was sure to be an unpopular message, but God was not so sympathetic. God was ready to enable and empower his newly called spokesman, but Moses continued to give the Lord one excuse after another.

Moses, like us, was quick to focus on his weaknesses, his fears, and his past failures. But God, as always, was ready to supply all that was needed for all he commanded. After Moses protested that he could not do the job because he was "not eloquent" and was "slow of speech", the Sovereign God put everything in perspective when he replied, "Who has made man's mouth? Who makes him mute, or deaf, or seeing, or blind? Is it not I, the Lord? Now therefore go, and I will be with your mouth" (Ex.4:10-12).

So the next time you feel reluctant, fearful or inadequate to do what you know Scripture calls you to do, remember that God will always supply what is needed as you step up with faith and obedience to do what he commands.

Resolve 39

*I will focus on what God calls me to do and trust him to enable me,
refusing to make excuses or focus on my own weaknesses.*

Unsung Heroes

So receive him in the Lord with all joy,
and honor such men
Philippians 2:29

Epaphroditus is one of the many unsung heroes of the Bible. His name means "attractive". And while we don't know anything about his physical appearance, when we read the New Testament we quickly discover that he possessed a beautiful character.

While others were abandoning the Apostle Paul in droves, Epaphroditus remained his faithful and loyal friend. When the Apostles lamented the selfishness of those who clamored for the Christian spotlight, Epaphroditus was on the short list of those who truly cared for the welfare of others.

In stark contrast to the values of our day where self-preservation, recreation and relaxation are a top priority, Epaphroditus like Paul worked himself to the point of exhaustion for the cause of Christ. Some would have expected Paul to chide Epaphroditus for overextending himself, but instead Paul praised him as an exemplary servant of Jesus Christ.

Lastly, and perhaps most importantly, when it comes to individuals with attractive and godly hearts like Epaphroditus, we must be sure that they are not unsung. Paul writes of him in Philippians 2:29, "honor such men!" So when you find a modern-day Epaphroditus, be sure he or she is not an obscure or unsung character in the story of your life.

Resolve 40

I will identify and sincerely honor those who exemplify a godly and attractive Christian character.

The Impotence of Worry

*Therefore do not be anxious about tomorrow,
for tomorrow will be anxious for itself.
Sufficient for the day is its own trouble.*
Matthew 6:34

Jesus regularly chided his disciples for their worry and anxiety. Worldly concerns about "what bad things might happen to us" are not befitting for followers of Christ.

The ultimate and eternal dangers, in our case, have been solved and settled by God's grace and Christ's finished work. Our relationship with him is unaffected by the hazards, risks or perils which lie around the next bend in life. After all, as Jesus often said, there is nothing that can be done about most things we tend to worry about. "And which of you by being anxious," Christ asked, "can add a single hour to his span of life? If then you are not able to do as small a thing as that, why are you anxious about the rest?" (Lk.12:25-26).

God sovereignly holds tomorrow's pains and pleasures, failures and victories in his omnipotent hand. Of course God wants us fully engaged in life – but it's the life right now he wants us focused on, not the potential "what ifs" that lie ahead (Mt.6:34).

So exercise your faith in a powerful God who sits enthroned over your future. Trust him, and let the hourly use of your faith drive out any anxiety concerning tomorrow.

Resolve 41

*I will choose to see worry for what it is – an offense to God
and a complete waste of my time.*

Fickle Feelings

*For the commandment is a lamp and the teaching a light,
and the reproofs of discipline are the way of life*
Proverbs 6:23

Our feelings are fickle but God's word is unchanging. There may be several factors, righteous and otherwise, which will influence our emotions, yet the Bible stands as our unalterable source of divine information, providing eternal clarity regarding God's values and priorities. This is why the Bible must serve as our perpetual guide for decision-making.

God repeatedly warns us to "not lean on our own understanding" (Pr.3:5) but instead to affirm with David that God's word is "a lamp to our feet and a light to our path" (Ps.119:105). It is tragic that much of modern Christianity has advocated a shift from objectively thinking our way through the Christian life in the light of God's written word, to subjectively feeling our way through the Christian life, being pushed and prodded by our fluctuating emotional impulses. How many clear passages of Scripture are ignored because Christians don't "feel it"? How many express commands in the Bible are disobeyed because God's people don't "feel led"? This should never be.

We must act on God's inscribed directives, not our shifting sentiments. So may we all reaffirm the historic Christian resolve to subject the entirety of our lives to the authority of God's word, even when our feelings are left to catch up.

Resolve 42

*I will trust Christ as I biblically think through my daily decisions,
instead of relying on my feelings and emotions.*

A Respectful Defense

But in your hearts honor Christ the Lord as holy, always being prepared to make a defense to anyone who asks you for a reason for the hope that is in you; yet do it with gentleness and respect
1 Peter 3:15

First Peter 3:15 commands all Christians to stand up for the truth and defend the hope of the gospel. It also commands that this be done with "gentleness and respect."

Unfortunately, there is something about defending the truth that can quickly deteriorate into heated arguments, belittling statements, and insulting remarks. It shouldn't. God expects his ambassadors to stay in control of their emotions and maintain a godly decorum that is worthy of their stately King. Christ's victory is already settled. His triumphant return is not dependent on our frenzied quarrels. The truth is settled. Christ has already won. Our objective is to provide dignified and respectful corrections to those who call his truth into question.

While our emotional disturbance is understandable when people malign our God, the Spirit's goal in our speech is "love, joy, peace, patience, kindness, goodness, faithfulness gentleness and self-control" (Gal.5:22-23). It may seem paradoxical, but we are called to fight for the truth gently and respectfully.

So don't get out there and attempt to defend Christ's honor in a dishonorable way. Keep your cool, and let your defense be seasoned with the courtesy and dignity that befits God's royal family.

Resolve 43

I will not let my emotions lead me to speak disrespectfully when defending the truth of Christ.

Misplaced Compassion

Do not be deceived: God is not mocked,
for whatever one sows, that will he also reap.
Galatians 6:7

Modern Christians tend to misplace a good portion of their compassion. Often when they learn of someone who is struggling or hurting, regardless of the reason, they are quick to offer their blessings, support and encouragement. This kind of indiscriminate sympathy is far from what we see in the pages of the New Testament.

The apostles maintained a careful distinction between "suffering for doing good" and "suffering for doing evil" (1Pt.3:13-17). The former is commended and Christians are called to offer their prayers and their reassuring help (1Pt.2:19-20). The latter calls for correction and usually prompted a godly rebuke (1Pt.4:14-17). When we fail to make this distinction we risk being supportive of the unrepentant, thus encouraging insensitive consciences and hardened hearts toward God (Heb.12:5-6). Or it could be that our aimless affirmations will unwittingly contribute to "mocking God" by glossing over the important relationship between "sowing and reaping" (Gal.6:7).

So when the connection between suffering and sin is obvious, we should pray and exhort the repentant sufferer to affirm God's holiness, and with David sing: "I know, O Lord, that your rules are righteous, and that in faithfulness you have afflicted me" (Ps.119:75). We all have much to learn from our self-inflicted trials. May we be quick to repent and learn our lessons so that we can make a full recovery and move on to walking even more closely with Christ.

Resolve 44

I will choose to be more discerning to see the difference between just and unjust suffering and seek to respond biblically.

—— The Real Problem with Sin ——

For we must all appear before the judgment seat of Christ,
so that each one may receive what is due for what he
has done in the body, whether good or evil.
2 Corinthians 5:10

At its core, the problem with sin has much less to do with the act itself, and much more to do with the fact that any commission of sin is a rebellion against God's authority. In our pragmatic world, that is an increasingly rare perspective.

Every day we hear Christians attempting to justify, defend or vindicate "biblical commands" because "God's ways are best for us" or because "doing things God's way works." The typical youth sermon, for instance, attempts to curry obedience to God's command against fornication by extrapolating its advantages for one's future marriage, or its guarantee against sexually transmitted diseases. Or consider the daily Christian talk shows which attempt to vindicate God's prohibition regarding homosexuality by trying to articulate this as a safeguard for "traditional family" and society, or by attempting to demonstrate the benefit of two-gender parenting.

But think back for a minute to the original sin. If pragmatism is the standard for obeying God's unambiguous commands, then Satan presented a legitimate argument for disobedience (Gen.3:2-6). The "forbidden fruit" was sinful, not because it was "bad", but simply because it was "forbidden". Sin isn't wrong because it's inherently bad for us (though it often is). Sin is bad because it is a direct act of rebellion against the God who has the authority and right to make the rules.

So look beyond the pragmatic rationale for upholding God's express commands. Recognize instead, that no matter what God has commanded, it matters little how advantageous it may or may not be to keep his commands, he is Lord and we are not, and one day we must all give an account for what we have done with his instructions (2Cor.5:10-11).

—————————————— Resolve 45 ——

I will choose to see sin more in terms of what it is before God
and less in terms of how it might negatively impact me.

Restraining Young Sinners

*Fathers, do not provoke your children to anger, but bring them
up in the discipline and instruction of the Lord.*
Ephesians 6:4

Parenting is hard work. Particularly because we are called by God to direct and correct young human beings who are born sinners (Ps.51:5), by nature chafe against the instructions of God (Rom.8:7; 1Cor.2:14), and are obstinately focused on pleasing their own selfish appetites (Eph.2:3). And yet, even from the youngest of years, this work to curtail, limit, shape and redirect young rebellious lives is precisely what God requires us to do (Eph.6:4; Pr.22:15).

Of course, our ultimate goal is to bring them to a mature understanding of the gospel of Jesus Christ, but at the same time, throughout each season of immaturity our job is to reign in, curb and restrain their innate impulses to do what is sinful (1Sam.3:13). For even before the transforming work of regeneration takes place, "a child makes himself known by his acts" (Pr.20:11) and parents are evaluated by either the submission or the insubordination of their children (Tit.1:6). And considering the great personal costs to your child for his or her moral choices (Gal.6:8), it makes sense that a mom or dad's effort in this task is seen as the definitive measure of parental love (Pr.13:24). It should come as no surprise that when permissiveness characterizes a home, shame, regret and disgrace will surely follow (Pr.29:15).

So if you are in the throes of correcting and corralling young sinners, take heart, your consistent, firm and loving discipline will reap a harvest of peace and righteousness (Pr.29:17).

Resolve 46

*I will take the task of parenting seriously and pray for those who are
entrusted with the privilege of directing young lives.*

The Authoritative Voice

Trust in the LORD with all your heart,
and do not lean on your own understanding.
In all your ways acknowledge him,
and he will make straight your paths.
Proverbs 3:5-6

Without an unswerving resolve to affirm that God has inscribed his authoritative voice on the pages of Scripture we are hopelessly lost on a turbulent sea of speculation and opinion. Isaiah cries out to those who subjectively look inward or elsewhere for answers and says, "to the law and to the testimony" for "should not a people inquire of their God?" (8:19-20). The familiar words of Proverbs 3:5 exhort: "Trust in the Lord with all your heart and do not lean on your own understanding".

Unfortunately for many Christians this means nothing more than subjectively imagining what God's input might be. But we need the objectivity of Scripture and not the subjectivity of our speculation. Subjectivity was the low point of biblical history. Remember the closing words of Judges, "and everyone did what was right in his own eyes" (Jdg.21:25b). We must value and consult God's written word if we are to claim his wisdom and direction.

Trusting in him and not ourselves means that we exalt his inspired sentences above our feelings and our impressions about what his thoughts might be. As the Psalmist often affirmed, "I shall have an answer… for I trust in your word" (119:42).

Resolve 47

I will value God's objective word above my feelings
and impressions.

Honest About Anxiety

Rejoice in the Lord always; again I will say, rejoice. Let your reasonableness be known to everyone. The Lord is at hand; do not be anxious about anything, but in everything by prayer and supplication with thanksgiving let your requests be made known to God. And the peace of God, which surpasses all understanding, will guard your hearts and your minds in Christ Jesus. Finally, brothers, whatever is true, whatever is honorable, whatever is just, whatever is pure, whatever is lovely, whatever is commendable, if there is any excellence, if there is anything worthy of praise, think about these things.
Philippians 4:4-8

When God confronts the sin of anxiety in Philippians 4, his prescribed remedy helps to clearly diagnose the problem - especially in the lives of those who tend to downplay its repercussions and choose to think that worry is not that big of a deal.

In Philippians 4:4-8 the Lord commands five things for those who are anxious and worried. He directs them to rejoice, to be reasonable, to remember Christ's return, to pray, and to consistently ponder good things. Consider how God's fix may in fact reveal the depth of our entanglement in this sin.

If you rarely find yourself spontaneously "rejoicing" and your heart is running low on joy, then maybe you are more worried and anxious than you care to admit. If you can detect that your interaction with others is often less than reasonable, then maybe anxiety has found a home in your heart. If your mind doesn't regularly turn to the victorious hope of Christ's second coming, if your prayer life is lagging, and if your thoughts don't persistently settle on what is honorable, pure and commendable, then it may be time to admit the root problem.

As with any sin, recognizing it and confessing it is the first step. Then we can move on to thoughtfully and purposefully employ these five inspired correctives. God is more than ready to give us victory over this destructive sin and to "guard our hearts and minds" (v.7) as we confess our sin and respond obediently to his instructions.

Resolve 48

I will be honest about the presence of worry and anxiety in my life and I will be quick to confess it and repent.

An Inevitable Reality

Jesus said, "Truly, I say to you, there is no one who has left house or brothers or sisters or mother or father or children or lands, for my sake and for the gospel, who will not receive a hundredfold now in this time, houses and brothers and sisters and mothers and children and lands, with persecutions, and in the age to come eternal life.
Mark 10:29-30

Many of us secretly hope that becoming Christians won't affect our preexisting friendships. But the natural and necessary division that Jesus promised is inescapable (Mt.10:34-37; Lk.12:51). Yes, we will still, like Jesus, lovingly reach out with the message of the gospel to our "old friends" (Eph.5:11-16), but our intimates and confidants will be exchanged for those who love and worship Christ.

To fight this inevitable reality is as futile as marrying the woman you adore and having your "old friends" chronically belittle, malign, misrepresent, misquote and insult her (which is what non-Christians do to Christ every day, if not with their words with their attitudes, values and allegiances). How could a man claim to value and cherish the relationship with his wife above all other human relationships, and passively endure her disparagement by his "old friends"?

It's not that we end our old set of relationships by some declaration or decree, but when we consistently stand up for Christ and his honor, when we urgently call our non-Christian friends to "Wake up!" and embrace Christ (Eph.5:14), those "old friends" have a way of either repenting of their sins or backing away – sometimes in dramatic fashion.

But don't despair. When non-Christians abandon us because of our allegiance to Christ, God has a terrific and caring way of replacing these important relationships with new friends who are sold-out to following Christ (Mk.10:28-30).

Resolve 49

I will value my relationship with Christ as more important than any other earthly relationship.

Pay Attention

I appeal to you therefore, brothers, by the mercies of God, to present your bodies as a living sacrifice, holy and acceptable to God, which is your spiritual worship. Do not be conformed to this world, but be transformed by the renewal of your mind, that by testing you may discern what is the will of God, what is good and acceptable and perfect.
Romans 12:1-2

Hebrews 2:1 tells us that "we must pay much closer attention to what we have heard, lest we drift away from it." Much like a leisurely float down a meandering river, if we choose to relax in the Christian life we can be assured that the tide of our culture and the tug of our flesh will draw our hearts and minds away from God's truth and further down the stream of unbelief and compromise.

The world we live in and the bodies we are encased in are not neutral. They persistently and actively work against the desires of our regenerate hearts and the righteous convictions of God's Spirit. This is why the Bible says to "present your bodies as living sacrifices, holy and acceptable to God" and to "not be conformed to this world, but be transformed by the renewal of your mind" (Rom.12:1-2). This is an active, focused, thoughtful work to "pay close attention" to God's truth. And it is needful because our regenerate heart is designed to be continually "renewed in knowledge after the image of its creator" (Col.3:10).

So with your full "attention" dive back into the life-changing "knowledge" you find in God's word and allow your mind to be "renewed", so that "by testing you may discern what is the will of God, what is good and acceptable and perfect" (Rom.12:2).

Resolve 50

I will purpose to fight the good fight of faith and pay closer attention to the truth I have learned.

— Remember to Whom You Pray —

The LORD has established his throne in the heavens,
and his kingdom rules over all.
Psalm 103:19

We need to remember the greatness of the God to whom we pray. We often pray small prayers for small things because we've forgotten the transcendent majesty of our God. Far too often, our perspective is trivial, temporal, and insignificant because we rush to our requests without considering just how "hallowed" his Name actually is (Mt.6:9).

When Nehemiah prayed for the challenges he faced, he reminded himself that he "prayed before the God of heaven" (1:4). Prior to laying his supplications before God he addressed him as "Yahweh, God of heaven, the great and awesome God" (1:5). It is good for us to say with Jeremiah, "Ah, Lord God! It is you who have made the heavens and the earth by your great power and by your outstretched arm! Nothing is too hard for you" (32:17). As God himself has said, "Every beast of the forest is mine" and even "the cattle on a thousand hills" (Ps.50:10).

So maybe our prayer list needs an overdue adjustment that comes from remembering that when we pray we are addressing the all-powerful, all-sufficient, everlasting King who has, and always will have, the ability to do whatever he chooses to do (Ps.115:3). So pray big, mindful that he "is able to do far more abundantly than all that we ask or think" (Eph.3:20).

Resolve 51

Before I ask God for anything I will remember his transcendent greatness and majesty.

Trusting in Christ

Therefore, we are ambassadors for Christ, God making his appeal
through us. We implore you on behalf of Christ, be reconciled to God.
For our sake he made him to be sin who knew no sin, so that in
him we might become the righteousness of God.
2 Corinthians 5:20-21

The Bible tells us that "the wages of sin is death" (Romans 6:23). Jesus came to solve both problems – sin and death! Sin was paid for at the cross on that dark Friday afternoon. Death was conquered at the empty tomb early on Sunday morning.

The point of the gospel is to have the payment of the cross applied to your sin, as you genuinely repent of your sin and wholeheartedly place your trust in Jesus Christ as the complete solution to the debt your sins have racked up against a holy God.

Don't fall to history's most frequent religious error, thinking that being good, sincere, or better than the next guy will somehow be a sin-canceling credit. We need to see our lives, including whatever perceived credits we might think we have, exchanged completely for the life, death, and resurrection of Christ.

Be sure your hope is in him and not yourself. Turn from sin and trust him today.

Resolve 52

I will trust Christ fully and remember that my acceptance before
God has been secured by him and not me.